Amazing Flying Machines

EYEWITNESS JUNIORS

Amazing Flying Machines

WRITTEN BY
ROBIN KERROD

PHOTOGRAPHED BY
MIKE DUNNING

ALFRED A. KNOPF • NEW YORK

Conceived and produced by
Dorling Kindersley Limited

Editor Bernadette Crowley
Art editor Toni Rann
Senior art editor Julia Harris
Senior editor Helen Parker
Production Shelagh Gibson

Illustrations by Peter Dennis, John Hutchinson and Julie Anderson
Flying machines supplied by Stanford Hall (pp 8-9); The Shuttleworth Collection (pp 12-13, 14-15);
The Science Museum (pp 16-17); Robert Willies (pp 18-19); CSE Aviation Limited (pp 20-21);
Robert Synge (pp 22-23); Pegasus Flight Training (pp 24-25); Fleet Air Arm Museum (pp 26-27)
Editorial consultant David Learmount
Special thanks to Carl Gombrich for research, and to Colonel Aubrey-Fletcher, Jane Hodgekins,
Daryl Molyneux, Peter Symes, and David Young for their help in finding the flying machines for photography.

The publishers would like to thank the following for their kind permission to reproduce
the photographs: Aviation Picture Library/Austin J. Brown (p 11); NASA (pp 28-29)

This is a Borzoi Book published by Alfred A. Knopf, Inc.

First American edition, 1992
All rights reserved under International and Pan-American Copyright Conventions.
Published in the United States by Alfred A. Knopf, Inc., New York.
Distributed by Random House, Inc., New York.
Published in Great Britain by Dorling Kindersley Limited, London.
Manufactured in Italy 0 9 8 7 6 5 4 3 2 1

Library of Congress Cataloging in Publication Data
Kerrod, Robin.
Amazing flying machines / written by Robin Kerrod.
p. cm. – (Eyewitness juniors; 18)
Includes index.
Summary: Text and photographs present flying machines throughout
history, including hot-air balloons, helicopters, and the space shuttle.

1. Airplanes – Juvenile literature. 2. Flying machines – Juvenile
literature [1. Airplanes – History. 2.. Flight – History.]
I. Title. II. Series.
TL547.K395 1992 629.13–dc20 91-53137
ISBN 0-679-82765-X
ISBN 0-679-92765-4 (lib. bdg.)

Color reproduction by Colourscan, Singapore
Printed in Italy by A. Mondadori Editore, Verona

Contents

Taking to the air

People dreamed about flying long before there were airplanes and other flying machines. They even tried strapping wings to their arms and flapping them like a bird.

The Hawk *is 24.5 ft from wing tip to wing tip*

Pilcher's *Hawk*

This glider, the *Hawk*, was one of the first successful flying machines. It was designed in 1898 by Percy Pilcher, who made many flights in it. But one day while flying, Pilcher had a fatal accident when one of the tail rods snapped.

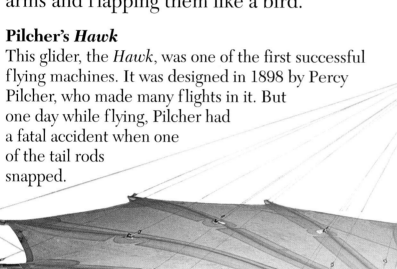

Cloth wings

Frame made of bamboo

Pedal flapper

Flying fascinated the Italian artist and inventor Leonardo da Vinci. In the 15th century he designed this human-powered machine with flapping wings. It was never built and would have been too heavy to fly.

Melting moment

In ancient Greek legend, Daedalus and his son Icarus escaped from prison by flying away with wings made of feathers and wax. But Icarus flew too close to the sun, and the wax melted. The wings broke up, and he plunged to his death.

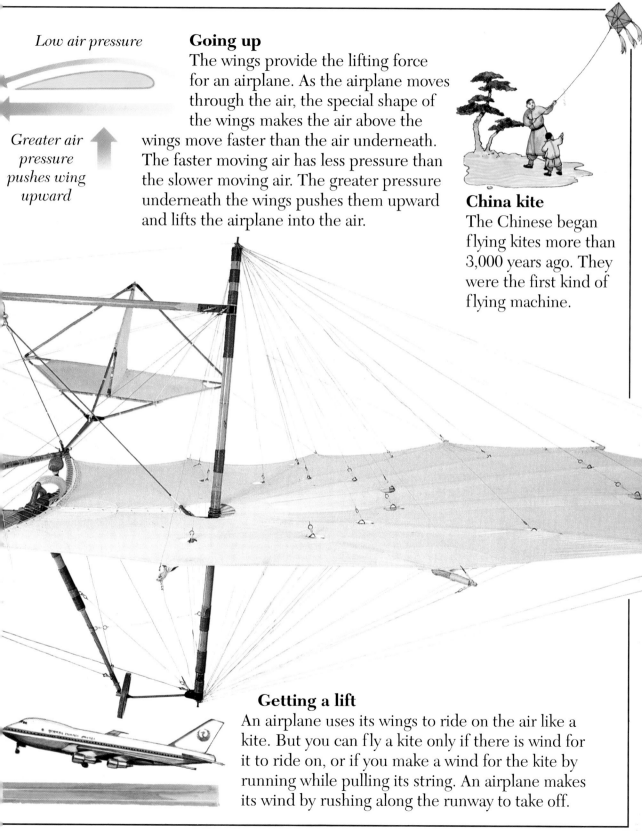

Low air pressure

Greater air pressure pushes wing upward

Going up

The wings provide the lifting force for an airplane. As the airplane moves through the air, the special shape of the wings makes the air above the wings move faster than the air underneath. The faster moving air has less pressure than the slower moving air. The greater pressure underneath the wings pushes them upward and lifts the airplane into the air.

China kite

The Chinese began flying kites more than 3,000 years ago. They were the first kind of flying machine.

Getting a lift

An airplane uses its wings to ride on the air like a kite. But you can fly a kite only if there is wind for it to ride on, or if you make a wind for the kite by running while pulling its string. An airplane makes its wind by rushing along the runway to take off.

Balloons and airships

Balloons were the first successful flying machines. A balloon will fly if it is filled with something lighter than the air around it. When a balloon is attached to an engine, it is called an airship.

Beautiful balloon

On October 15, 1783, François de Rozier became the first human to fly – in this balloon built by the Montgolfier brothers. Montgolfier balloons flew because they were filled with hot air, and hot air is lighter than cold air.

Farmyard flight

On September 19, 1783, a rooster, a duck, and a sheep crowed, quacked, and baaed their way into the history books. They became the first living creatures to fly. They took off from Versailles, France, in a balloon built by Joseph and Etienne Montgolfier.

Riding high

In 18th-century France, balloon flights were often an attraction at festivals. In 1798, Henri Margat entertained the crowd when he sat on his white stag Coco, for a balloon ride across Paris.

Gas balloon

A scientist named Jacques Charles built a different kind of balloon. He filled it with hydrogen, the lightest gas there is. On December 1, 1783, he and Ainé Robert took off from Paris, France, and traveled 25 miles

Steerable steamer

Balloons can go only where the wind blows them. In 1852, however, Frenchman Henri Giffard fitted a steam engine to a balloon so the balloon could be steered. It was the first airship.

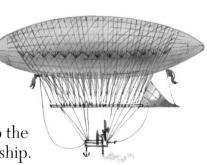

This balloon is about 65 ft high

The balloon is made out of nylon

Airship explosion

Count Ferdinand von Zeppelin of Germany made the most famous airships. The Zeppelin *Hindenburg* was the world's largest airship, with a length of 804 ft, but it was destroyed by fire when landing in 1937.

Balloons are back

Balloons were almost forgotten as the airplane was developed. But recently they have become popular again. This modern balloon is being lifted by hot air, just like the very first balloon.

11

Powered flight

The first winged flying machines with engines took to the skies in the early 1900s. They were called airplanes, a word that means "wanderers in the air." The daring pilots who flew these flimsy machines were called aviators, or "birdmen."

Flies like a stone

There were all sorts of wacky inventions, even after the secret of powered flight was discovered. This plane from 1908 couldn't lift off the ground.

Wired together

Early planes, like this Deperdussin, were built of wood and fabric and were held together by wires.

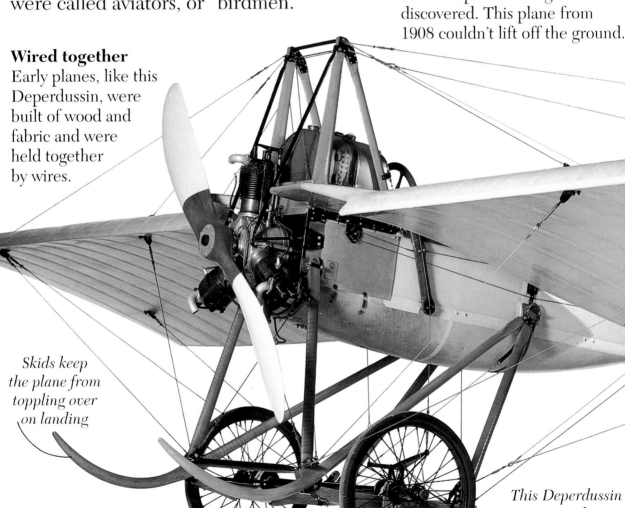

Skids keep the plane from toppling over on landing

This Deperdussin is 24.6 ft long and has a wingspan of 28.5 ft

This Deperdussin is a monoplane – a plane with one set of wings

Getting it Wright

In 1903, Orville and Wilbur Wright attached propellers and a gasoline engine to a glider and called it *Flyer*. Orville flew the machine for 12 seconds. It was the world's first airplane flight.

Taking a dive

In 1898, the U.S. government gave Samuel Langley money to make the world's first successful powered aircraft. He did not succeed. His plane, called an "aerodrome," dived off its launch platform into the river on takeoff – twice.

In all weathers

Most early aviators had little protection from the wind and rain, but none had less than pilots of *Antoinette* monoplanes. They sat on the planes instead of in them!

French crossing

In Europe the French were the first to go crazy over flying. On July 25, 1909, Louis Blériot made the first airplane crossing of the English Channel in his plane *Blériot X1*.

Winged wonders

In the early years of flying, most airplanes had two sets of wings and were called biplanes. Some airplanes had three sets of wings. These were called triplanes.

Flying camel

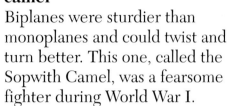

Biplanes were sturdier than monoplanes and could twist and turn better. This one, called the Sopwith Camel, was a fearsome fighter during World War I.

Dogfights

World War I (1914–1918) was the first war in which fighting took place in the air. Pilots figured out all kinds of tactics to get the better of their enemies. They would make sharp turns and rolls during combat, in what came to be called dogfights.

Red for danger

One of the best German planes was the Fokker triplane. Ace pilot Manfred von Richthofen flew a red one. He became known as the Red Baron and was one of the most successful fighter pilots of World War I.

K
3215

K 3215

Rudder helps turn the airplane sideways

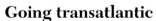

Going transatlantic

The first nonstop crossing of the Atlantic was made in June 1919 by John Alcock and Arthur Whitten Brown. They started their historic journey from the U.S., flying a Vickers Vimy biplane. They landed 16 hours later – nose down in a bog in Ireland!

Stairway to heaven
Horatio Phillips's multiplane from the 1890s has so many wings, it looks more like a ladder than an airplane!

Maiden voyage
There have been many daring women pilots. In 1930, Amy Johnson became the first woman to fly solo from England to Australia. She flew her Gypsy Moth biplane, *Jason*, in a journey lasting 20 days.

The Avro Tutor was 26 ft long and had a wingspan of 34 ft

Flying school
This 1931 airplane, the Avro Tutor, made a few twists and turns in its time. It was used for training air force pilots.

Sea dog
Commander E. Dunning, flying a Sopwith Pup, made the first landing on a moving ship in 1917. He tried to repeat the landing a week later, but a strong wind blew the plane overboard, and he was killed.

Passenger planes

People began flying in large numbers in the early 1930s. Passenger planes, or airliners, then took on a new look. They were built of metal and had a sleek design, much like the airliners of today.

Metal bird

In the late 1920s, airplane makers started building airplanes out of aluminum, a silver-colored metal, instead of wood and fabric. The Ford Tri-motor passenger plane of 1926 was one of the first successful metal airplanes. It was known as the "Tin Goose."

Bumpy rides

The first airliners flew low and were shaken about in the swirling air currents. Passengers often had a rough ride. Sometimes their seats weren't even fixed to the floor!

The Lockheed 10-A Electra is 38 ft long

High office

In 1928, a de Havilland DH61 passenger plane was converted into an office by a newspaper company. It had a desk, a typewriter, a darkroom for developing photographs, and even a motorcycle so a reporter could get to an event quickly.

Boeing's beautiful bird

The Boeing 247, launched in 1933, was the first modern airliner. It had a smooth, streamlined shape, and after takeoff, its wheels folded up into the wing. All this made it slip through the air more easily.

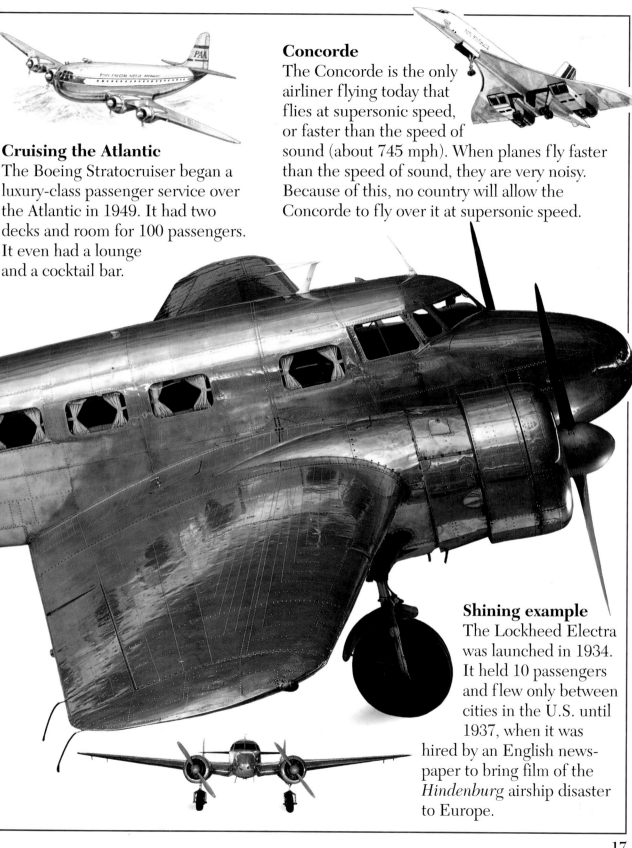

Cruising the Atlantic
The Boeing Stratocruiser began a luxury-class passenger service over the Atlantic in 1949. It had two decks and room for 100 passengers. It even had a lounge and a cocktail bar.

Concorde
The Concorde is the only airliner flying today that flies at supersonic speed, or faster than the speed of sound (about 745 mph). When planes fly faster than the speed of sound, they are very noisy. Because of this, no country will allow the Concorde to fly over it at supersonic speed.

Shining example
The Lockheed Electra was launched in 1934. It held 10 passengers and flew only between cities in the U.S. until 1937, when it was hired by an English newspaper to bring film of the *Hindenburg* airship disaster to Europe.

Seaplanes

Seaplanes take off and land on water. There are three types: a floatplane has floats instead of wheels; a flying boat has a body shaped like the bottom of a boat; an amphibian is a flying boat that also has wheels for landing on the ground.

The engine is at the top of the airplane to keep water from entering it

First crossing

A month before Alcock and Brown made the first nonstop crossing of the Atlantic, a Curtiss NC-4 seaplane made the very first crossing of the Atlantic, from Canada to England. It made two stops on the way. The whole trip took 53 hours and 58 minutes.

Amphibian

The Lake Buccaneer is an amphibian. When landing on water, its wheels are sealed inside watertight doors. It even has an anchor for mooring.

Watertight door for front wheel

Watery runway

In the early 1930s, airlines preferred to use seaplanes on long-distance routes since they could land in places where there were no airports or landing strips – provided there was water, of course!

Float sits on water to keep wing above water

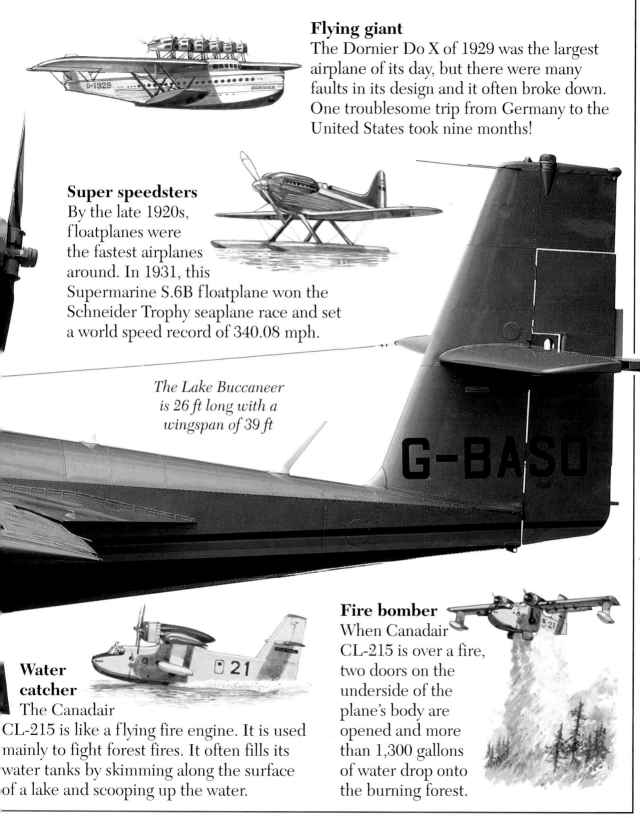

Flying giant
The Dornier Do X of 1929 was the largest airplane of its day, but there were many faults in its design and it often broke down. One troublesome trip from Germany to the United States took nine months!

Super speedsters
By the late 1920s, floatplanes were the fastest airplanes around. In 1931, this Supermarine S.6B floatplane won the Schneider Trophy seaplane race and set a world speed record of 340.08 mph.

The Lake Buccaneer is 26 ft long with a wingspan of 39 ft

G-BASO

Fire bomber
When Canadair CL-215 is over a fire, two doors on the underside of the plane's body are opened and more than 1,300 gallons of water drop onto the burning forest.

Water catcher
The Canadair CL-215 is like a flying fire engine. It is used mainly to fight forest fires. It often fills its water tanks by skimming along the surface of a lake and scooping up the water.

Spinning wings

The helicopter is a most remarkable flying machine. Not only can it fly forward, but it can fly sideways and backward too. It can hover in the air like a hawk, and it takes off and lands straight up and down.

The tail rotor keeps the helicopter from spinning around as the main rotor blades spin

Maple spinners

A maple seed has wings that act like a helicopter's rotor blades. When a seed falls from a tree, its wings make it spin, keeping it up in the air longer.

G-BS

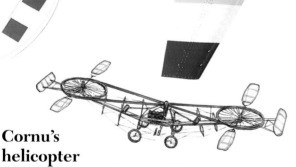

Cornu's helicopter

This helicopter, designed by Frenchman Paul Cornu, made the very first helicopter flight in 1907. All it did was lift 6 ft off the ground and stay there for 20 seconds!

Super-copters!

The helicopter is ideal for rescuing people from tricky places. So if you're ever shipwrecked – don't panic! Chances are you'll be picked up by an air-sea rescue helicopter.

Windmill wing

An autogyro is like a helicopter, but its rotor blades are moved by the air, not by an engine. As the machine moves forward, the passing air forces the rotor blades to spin, lifting the machine into the air.

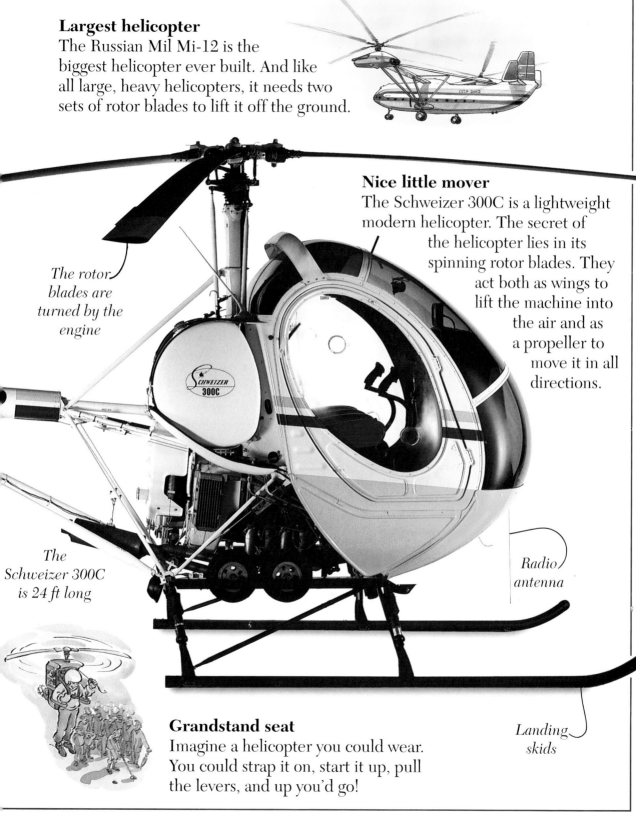

Largest helicopter
The Russian Mil Mi-12 is the biggest helicopter ever built. And like all large, heavy helicopters, it needs two sets of rotor blades to lift it off the ground.

Nice little mover
The Schweizer 300C is a lightweight modern helicopter. The secret of the helicopter lies in its spinning rotor blades. They act both as wings to lift the machine into the air and as a propeller to move it in all directions.

The rotor blades are turned by the engine

The Schweizer 300C is 24 ft long

Radio antenna

Landing skids

Grandstand seat
Imagine a helicopter you could wear. You could strap it on, start it up, pull the levers, and up you'd go!

Aerobats

Aerobats are the acrobats of the air. Since the early days of flying, daredevil pilots have looped and rolled their planes in the sky to show off their skill and to thrill spectators.

Looping the loop

Flying circus
In the 1920s and 1930s, groups of pilots would travel from town to town to give spectacular flying shows. These bold pilots were known as barnstormers. In one of their stunts, a person walked along the aircraft wing – with no parachute!

This is one of the classic aerobatic movements. The plane goes into a dive to pick up speed and then climbs steeply. It then loops over backward, before diving again, right side up.

Radio antenna

Pitts
SPECIAL
S-2A

G-PIT

High kicks
The barnstorming craze reached Hollywood, the center of the movie industry in the 1930s. Hollywood's version of barnstorming was pure fantasy, though!

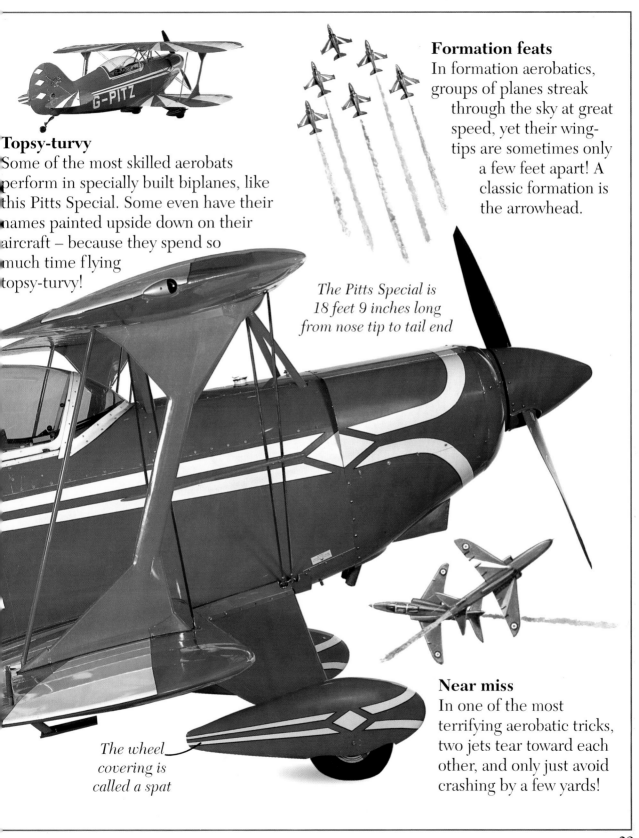

Topsy-turvy

Some of the most skilled aerobats perform in specially built biplanes, like this Pitts Special. Some even have their names painted upside down on their aircraft – because they spend so much time flying topsy-turvy!

Formation feats

In formation aerobatics, groups of planes streak through the sky at great speed, yet their wing-tips are sometimes only a few feet apart! A classic formation is the arrowhead.

The Pitts Special is 18 feet 9 inches long from nose tip to tail end

Near miss

In one of the most terrifying aerobatic tricks, two jets tear toward each other, and only just avoid crashing by a few yards!

The wheel covering is called a spat

Up, up, and away

Flying in light aircraft does not feel the same as being inside the strong body of a jumbo jet. Pilots are often out in the open, with no more than their clothes as covering. It's exciting, though perhaps a bit hair-raising!

Ultralight

An ultralight weighs no more than 330 lb, although it can fly as high as a jet plane. This ultralight can be packed up and carried inside a van. It can take off from a short track, or even a beach – provided there aren't sunbathers in the way!

This ultralight has a wingspan of 34 ft and a body length of 8 ft

Handgrip

Propeller

Engine

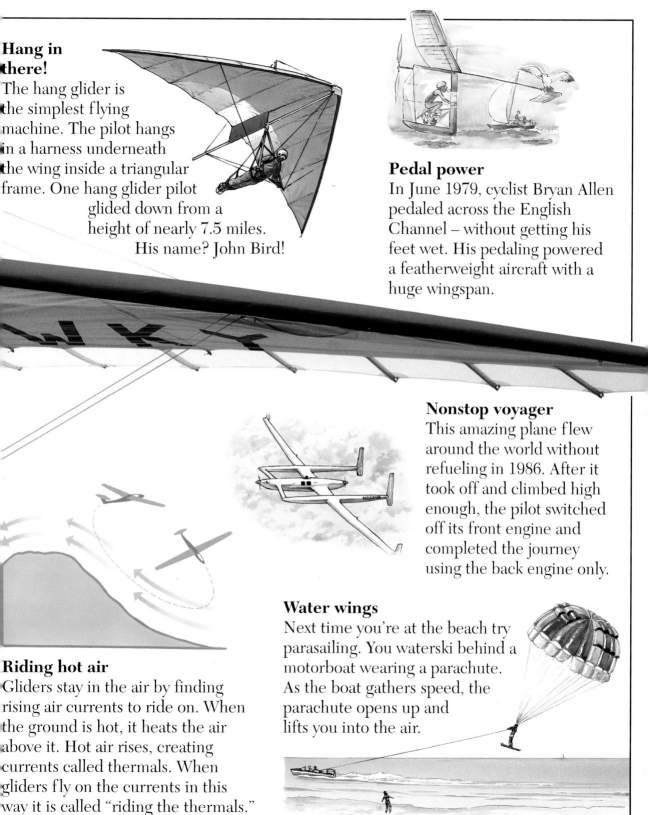

Hang in there!

The hang glider is the simplest flying machine. The pilot hangs in a harness underneath the wing inside a triangular frame. One hang glider pilot glided down from a height of nearly 7.5 miles. His name? John Bird!

Pedal power

In June 1979, cyclist Bryan Allen pedaled across the English Channel – without getting his feet wet. His pedaling powered a featherweight aircraft with a huge wingspan.

Nonstop voyager

This amazing plane flew around the world without refueling in 1986. After it took off and climbed high enough, the pilot switched off its front engine and completed the journey using the back engine only.

Riding hot air

Gliders stay in the air by finding rising air currents to ride on. When the ground is hot, it heats the air above it. Hot air rises, creating currents called thermals. When gliders fly on the currents in this way it is called "riding the thermals."

Water wings

Next time you're at the beach try parasailing. You waterski behind a motorboat wearing a parachute. As the boat gathers speed, the parachute opens up and lifts you into the air.

Jets

In the 1940s, airplanes without propellers began taking to the air. They were powered by jets of hot gases. Jet-driven airplanes can travel much faster than propeller airplanes – some jets can fly at more than three times the speed of sound.

Beating the barrier

In October 1947, the Bell X-1 rocket plane was the first airplane to fly faster than the speed of sound. It was flown by test pilot Chuck Yeager, who named the airplane *Glamorous Glennis*, after his wife.

Straight up

Helicopters were the first aircraft to take off and land vertically, or straight up and down. Now, vertical takeoff and landing (VTOL) is performed by special jets called jump jets. These jump jets can land in tricky places and on moving ships, just like helicopters.

WG774

Rising bed

The first jet-propelled vertical takeoff and landing was done by an experimental machine that looked like a big iron bed. And it was called the Flying Bedstead!

The BAC-221 is 33 ft long

Turbo power

The simplest jet engine is called a turbojet. A compressor sucks air into the engine and forces it into a chamber, where it is mixed with fuel. This mixture burns and produces very hot gases, which expand rapidly. These gases spin a kind of windmill called a turbine, which turns the compressor. The hot gases then shoot out backward as a jet stream.

Compressor is like several rows of fans

Hot gases shoot out, causing turbine to spin

Jet stream thrusts airplane forward

Air intake

Fuel goes in here

Burning fuel and air mixture

The fastest

The Lockheed SR-71A Blackbird is the fastest aircraft ever to have flown. In 1976, it set a world record of 2,193 mph, which is more than three times the speed of sound.

Stealthy stalkers

Radar detects aircraft by sending out radio waves that bounce off the aircraft; an "echo" comes back to the radar receiver. But "stealth" planes, like this Northrop B-2A, are made of special materials, and are specially shaped, so that they absorb or scatter radar waves. Then no echo is received.

Blue jet

This sleek jet, the BAC-221, was built in 1960. It was used to research high-speed flight and could fly at supersonic speed. Many features of the BAC-221 were used in the Concorde's design.

Swinging wings

Some jet fighters have wings that can swing forward and back. The wings stick out sideways to takeoff and land slowly. But in flight the wings swing back. This allows the fighters to travel at very high speeds.

The final frontier

It is only recently that flying machines have rocketed into space. One of the latest spacecraft is the shuttle, which takes people and satellites into space. The satellites are left there to orbit Earth, but the people come back down again!

Five jumbos
The shuttle can carry heavy loads into space. It could carry five adult African elephants – if they could be squeezed in!

Shuttle movement
The space shuttle blasts away from the launch pad with the power of about 140 jumbo jets. But when it returns from space, it does not use engines – it is computer-controlled to land perfectly.

The shuttle lands on a runway like a glider

NASA

United States

Moon hop
In 1969, Neil Armstrong and Edwin Aldrin were the first people to set foot on the moon. Because there is very little gravity up there, they found it easier to hop than walk in their padded suits.

Falling apart

The shuttle lifts off with its three engines and two booster rockets blazing. After two minutes, the booster rockets fall away and parachute down. Six minutes later, the fuel tank, now empty, falls away. But by this time, the shuttle is in space.

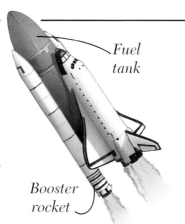

Fuel tank

Booster rocket

Hot stuff

When the shuttle returns from space, it shoots through the air at great speed. Pushing through the air so fast makes the shuttle red-hot. But the thick tiles on the outside keep the heat from getting inside.

Discovery

The tiles are made of silica

Nice to meet you!

We have no proof that life exists on other planets, but many people believe that alien creatures often pay us a visit.

Orient Express

This future U.S. spaceplane has been nicknamed the "Orient Express." It could be used one day as an airliner to whisk passengers from country to country at lightning speed.

Index